Predicting the Unpredictable

Pragmatic Approaches to Estimating Cost or Schedule

Johanna Rothman

Predicting the Unpredictable

Johanna Rothman

Published by Practical Ink
www.jrothman.com

Practical **ink**

Cover design by Brandon Swann

ISBN-13: 978-1-943487-00-4

*To everyone who was ever asked
"How much will this project cost?" or
"How long will this project take?"*

Contents

Troubleshooting Your Estimation Problems

Acknowledgments

I thank my Managing Product Development[1] blog readers. You asked me enough questions that I had to write the answers.

I thank my editors, Rebecca Airmet and Nancy Groth. I thank Jean Jesensky for her indexing. I thank Karen Billipp for her layout for the print book.

Any errors are mine.

---

[1] http://www.jrothman.com/blog/mpd/

CHAPTER 1

Introduction

One of the big questions in organizations is "How much will this project cost?" The other question is "When will this project be done?" In fact, the bigger the project, the more the people in the organization want to know.

The problem with these questions is that they are predictions. I don't know about you, but my crystal ball is opaque. It's never been good at predictions.

On the other hand, I've had pretty good results with educated guesses. I've had even better results with using data to update my guesses as I've proceeded.

Estimation has been a common "problem" in software projects. I have written about it in essays and blog posts for several years. I decided if I created a book, I could share what has worked for me, in real projects and programs. You could apply these ideas in your projects and programs.

1.1 Estimates Are Guesses or Predictions

We want accurate estimates. When I drive to a local appointment longer than 10 minutes away, I want to know how long it will take me to get there. I can use a mapping application to estimate my drive, given the current traffic.

I have driven to appointments only 14 miles away, and sometimes it takes me 20 minutes to drive. Sometimes, it takes me about an hour. That's a huge difference.

My general estimate is that I should give myself 20–25 minutes of driving time. But if I always planned on 25 minutes, I would be late—substantially late—about half the time.

We don't want that with our project estimates. And yet, we are "late" with projects.

When I drive to an appointment, I don't add features. We often add or change requirements with projects and expect the estimate to be the same as predicted.

I don't change who is driving—it's always me. Yet, we change people on teams and expect the estimate to be the same.

I don't multitask when I drive. Yet, we ask people to multitask and expect the estimate to be the same.

An initial project estimate is your best guess at the time you make the estimate. The accuracy of that estimate depends on the people doing the estimation and what they know about the project.

Your estimate is a guess, a prediction. It is not fact. If I have trouble estimating my driving time, which has far fewer variabilities than a project, how can you expect your project estimate to be accurate? You can't, not with the very first estimate you create. You can iterate on the estimate and make it better over time.

1.2 Estimates Change

As you proceed with your project, your estimate will change. Your estimate might change because:

- You know more about the project's features/requirements.
- The people understand how to work together.
- You have history with these people working on this project. That history will allow you to better your prediction.
- The project itself changes: adding, subtracting, and changing requirements as we learn more about what we can provide and more about what the customer desires.

Note that in my driving metaphor, my destination doesn't change—unless I abandon my drive! Because projects change, our first estimate is a guess or prediction. That's why it's so important to update your estimate as you proceed.

1.3 Estimates Expire

Not only can the project itself change, which changes the estimate, but estimates have an expiration date.

On an agile project, as you finish features, you learn more about the requirements. You learn what a Minimum Viable Product, MVP, is. You might need a Minimum Indispensable Feature Set[1] first, enabling you to create short features in flow or iterations.

If you work in a non-agile way, you will address risks—technical, schedule, or quality risks—and learn from them.

Regardless of your type of project, the estimate you create at the very beginning will expire. It is no longer valid.

Keep these ideas in mind as you read this book. These ideas are true regardless of your project's life cycle.

I've collected here what I've written over the years to provide guidance about estimation. I hope you use it and enjoy it.

---

[1] http://brodzinski.com/2014/12/minimal-indispensable-feature-set.html

CHAPTER 2

What Estimates Are

Managers and sponsors ask a project team for estimates all the time. Sometimes, managers use those estimates to plan which project to do first—which is a terrible idea. More on that later. Sometimes, managers use those estimates to predict a target date. Sometimes, managers use those estimates as a commitment.

None of those ways are the way we should use estimates.

Here is the problem with using estimates that way:

- Estimates expire.
- Estimates change.
- Estimates are guesses.

Yes, "guess" is the dictionary definition of estimate. The more you know about the domain, the requirements, and how the team works together, the more educated your guess will be. But it will still be a guess.

Because estimates are guesses, you can't use them for precise prediction until you get close to the event you are estimating.

You can spiral in on more accurate estimates. You can provide a percentage confidence on your estimate as you proceed through your work. You can change your estimate as you learn more about the necessary (and unnecessary) requirements.

2.1 Provide an Accurate but Not Precise Estimate

Can you have an accurate estimate at the beginning of a project? It depends. If the project is similar to what you have done before, with a team that is accustomed to working together, and the effort is short—say no longer than three months—you have a good chance of providing an accurate estimate.

For our purposes, an accurate estimate is one that is no more or less than 5–10% off the final effort.

If you have a 12-week effort, and you finished inside of a week either way, would you consider that a good estimate? I would. That's what I mean by an accurate estimate.

Instead, if you say, "We will finish on Wednesday, the 23rd at 5pm," would anyone believe you? They might, if you have an important demo or release scheduled for Wednesday, the 23rd at 6pm! That's a precise estimate.

Maybe, you use that precise date as a target, a predictive estimate. You timebox the work so you can finish it by that time. That's useful to do with trade shows, demos, and other events where you are not in charge of the date.

When someone asks you, "How long will the project take?" or "How much will the project cost?" they are not talking about a precise estimate. They want an accurate estimate. You need to know the difference.

To manage people's expectations, always report your estimate with a percentage confidence, a date range (optimistic, likely, pessimistic), or spiral in on a date.

Now that you know about the fallibility of estimates, let's consider why we estimate.

CHAPTER 3

Why Do We Estimate Anyway?

We estimate for these reasons:

- To provide an order-of-magnitude size/cost/date about the project, so we have a rough idea of the size/cost/date for planning purposes. An order-of-magnitude size means we want to invest just enough time in the estimate that we believe in the accuracy of it for planning purposes.
- We want to know when we will be done, because we are close.
- We need to allocate money or teams of people for some amount of time.
- Someone wants to know who to blame.

Creating a gross estimate can be useful. See Estimating the Unknown: Dates or Budgets (5.1, p. 16) to learn how. You can iterate on that estimate, especially as you get closer to completion.

A gross estimate with deliverable milestones can help the organization allocate money or teams for a while. The deliverable milestones help you know when you have completed enough value. The value is a compilation of features, something you can demo.

In fact, back when phase-gate (serial) life cycles were developed, estimation was key to a project's success.

After you completed a phase, you were supposed to re-estimate, in order to change what you did with the project.

Now, if you are using an incremental approach or an agile approach, you see completed work. And you don't have to re-estimate.

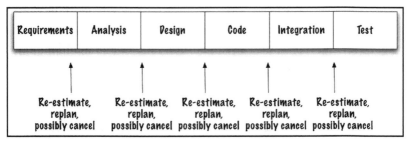

Role of Estimation in a Serial Life Cycle

However, you should be aware that many managers may be thinking about a serial life cycle when they ask for estimates.

3.1 Why Do You Estimate?

Why do *you* estimate? If you've estimated because you always have, think about it. If you estimate because your money people want to do once-a-year money allocation, well, you know that's fiction. You can do it without detailed project estimation.

For money allocation, decide how valuable the project is to you. When does the project have to deliver the value? Now, tell the project team when the value has to be delivered. That's all.

Remember, you hired these people because they were smart, responsible human beings. Stop with the phases and all that nonsense. Tell them what you want. Remember, the phases exist because management wanted to be able to cancel the project before it got too far along. You were supposed to show a deliverable and re-estimate at each phase. If you don't cancel or deliver something and re-estimate at each phase, your phases are not working for you.

Buy your team a copy of *Manage It! Your Guide to Modern, Pragmatic Project Management* (ROTPM), which explains how to manage projects in any life cycle. Give them a ranked backlog. Let them deliver. If they can't deliver in the money or date frame, they will tell you. They are responsible humans.

If you need an order-of-magnitude estimation, fine. That doesn't take days to determine. That takes hours. It will be precise-wrong and order-of-magnitude-right. Timebox your estimation effort. It's an order of magnitude. Don't hold anyone to that estimate. (Remember, estimates are guesses. They are not "The One and Only Truth.")

If you want to know when you'll be done because you think you're close to the end of the project, ask yourself this question: Is it worth the time to estimate versus the time to finish? It might be. But know you are taking time away from finishing.

And if you want to play the blame game, remember that management is the one who needs to shoulder the most blame. Why? Because management set the constraints. Don't believe me? Read Estimating the Unknown: Dates or Budgets (5.1, p. 16) now.

I can sympathize with management's need for estimates. I like order-of-magnitude estimates for many things. I even like specific estimates as we get closer. But creating software is not like driving somewhere or like constructing a building. When I drive somewhere, I do want step-by-step instructions. When constructing a building, I do want an estimate. And even then, I am pretty sure the estimate is optimistic.

When creating software, I want to see working software as we create it, because with working software, we learn. The learning is what's most important. Because once we've learned enough, we can stop. That's what's most valuable. Not the estimate.

3.2 Ask This Question Before You Estimate

When people ask you for your estimates, they are trying to determine the value of the project to the organization.

You can ask them to articulate their desires with either of these questions:

- How much do you want to invest before we stop?
- How much value is this project or program worth to you?

Start a conversation with your sponsor, so you can understand what is important to your sponsor. Once you do, you can decide what to do next. You may want a gross estimate, as in Estimating the Unknown: Dates or Budgets (5.1, p. 16). You may want to change your project approach, and do some up-front work to generate a more detailed estimate. You have choices.

CHAPTER 4

Software is Learning, Not Construction

Here's one problem I have with estimation. Software is not construction. We can't build software the same way we construct or manufacture something. Software is all about learning and innovating as a team. Some people think that software is invention. Whatever you think about software, it is *not* construction.

We can timebox our learning. We can choose to stop doing something. We can put acceptance or release criteria around it and say, "We have done enough for now."

But, we cannot say, "We can build this software for $xx per square foot." We don't know how to do that. Because we have not built exactly this software before. If we had built software like this before, we could estimate pretty darn close, because we either have historical data with good estimation quality, or we have small chunks of work we know about, or both.

(There are some tools, such as Cocomo, SLIM, and function point counting that ask you many questions at the start of your project to provide an estimate for the entire project. If you are not agile, you may want to consider those tools. Know that you will invest substantial time preparing for the estimate, time that takes you away from helping the team learn what to do or how to work together. The people who sell these tools and services are convinced they work. I am not.)

When we estimate, other people think of our estimates the way they think of estimates in other fields, especially construction.

Especially if you provide a single-point estimate. Even if you provide assumptions, which no one hears.

Software is nothing like construction. Software is innovation. Innovation is difficult—if not impossible—to predict.

Since software is about learning, and we rarely, if ever, do the same project twice, we are always estimating the unknown. That makes our estimates inaccurate.

There is an alternative to estimating.

Make your features small, as in something you can deliver in a day or so. You can also swarm over the work, so the team finishes a story every day. If you finish something each day, people can see your work product. They trust you. They stop asking you for estimates.

If you always have deliverable software—this includes all tests, documentation, everything you need—you don't need to estimate anything. You also gain the benefit of learning, so if someone asks, "How hard is this thing to do?" the entire team can huddle together for a few minutes and say, "It's this story and that story and this story, too."

They then say, "We know it's at least these three stories, and that's off the top of our heads. Are those stories more important than the ones at the top of our queue?"

4.1 Inch-Pebbles or Small Stories Show Progress

Because we learn when we write software, we need to show progress to ourselves and to our customers. Small features or small tasks show progress and build trust. It's also much easier to estimate something small than it is something large.

If you create small stories or inch-pebbles, you can track how long it took you to create those stories. Or, you can ask, "Is this story similar in size to that one?"

You learn about how large one or two days of work is. You want to know this. The smaller the granularity of stories or work, the easier it is to count them. You will have a more accurate estimate.

4.2 Learn With Spikes

Sometimes you have something you don't even know how to start estimating. You don't even know how to start the work. That's when you need a spike. See Spike It! (p. 81).

You timebox a short amount of time—say a day or less—and work with your team to determine what the next steps are. At the end of this timebox, you and the team probably know enough about the work to break it down to estimate it.

Take every opportunity to learn as you estimate. You will have a much more accurate estimate.

CHAPTER 5

Think About Estimation

First, remember that a project is a system. And, a system has multiple aspects.

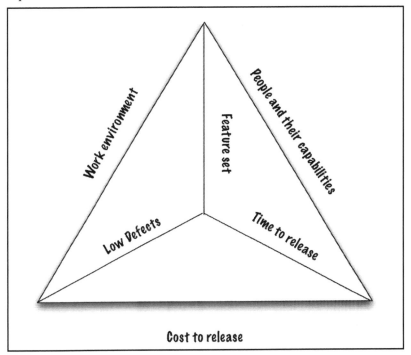

Project Pyramid

If you've been managing projects for a while, you know that there is no iron triangle. Instead, there is a project pyramid.

On the outside, there are the typical corporate constraints: Who will work on the project (the people and their capabilities), the work environment, and the cost to release. Most often, those are fixed by the organization. "Bud, we'll give you 50 people, 5 months, and this pile of money to go do that project. OK?"

The inside edges are what the customer wants: A specific feature set, at a reasonable level of quality by a certain date.

Whether or not it's okay, you're supposed to nod your head like a bobble-headed doll. But, if your management has not thought about the constraints, they may be asking you to smush more features than your people can accomplish in the allotted time, given the requested time to release, with the expected number of low defects and the expected cost to release.

The time to release is dependent on the number of people and their capabilities as well as the project environment. You can *make* anything work. You may have delays with geographically distributed teams, and even life cycles that do not include iteration with long lists of features.

This is why estimation of the budget or the time to release is so difficult. You have to consider the entire context.

5.1 Estimating the Unknown: Dates or Budgets

Almost every manager I know wants to know when a project will be done. Some managers decree when a project will be done. Some managers think they can decree both the date and the feature set. There is one other tiny small subset, those managers who ask, "When can you finish this set of ranked features?"

And, some managers want you to estimate the budget as well as the date. And now, you're off into la-la land. Look, if you had any predictive power, you'd be off somewhere gambling, making a ton of money. But, you do have options. All of them require iterating on the estimates and the project.

First, a couple of cautions:

1. Never, ever, ever provide a single date for a project or a single point for a budget without a range or a confidence level.

2. Expect to iterate on the release date and on the budget, and train your managers to expect iterative, improved estimates from you.

3. If you get a ranked feature set, you can provide working product in the order in which your managers want the work done, while you keep refining your estimates. This has to be good for everyone.

4. If you can say this without being patronizing, practice saying, "Remember, the definition of estimate is guess."

So now that you know why it's so difficult to estimate, what do you do when someone asks you for an estimate?

5.2 Determine Your Degrees of Freedom

First, you ask a question back: "What's most important to you? Imagine it's three weeks before our desired release date. We don't have all the features done. We have more defects than we wanted. What do you want to do?"

- If they say, "Features. Finish the features," then you need to optimize for finishing features. You have to manage technical risk. Features are driving your project.
- If they say, "Date. If we don't make the date, we are toast," then you know you have to timebox everything so you meet the date with completed work. The release date is driving the project.
- If they say, "Cost," then you know to manage the run rate. Make sure people aren't multitasking. Cost-to-release is the driver.
- If they say, "Low defects," then you know you need the team to complete one feature at a time before they start anything else. Low defects is the driver.

If you review the Project Pyramid, you can see that everything depends on everything else. However, in each project or program, you only have one #1 priority. That priority is either the release date, the feature set, the cost-to-release, or a low defect count. Your management might want to contain costs or use certain people, or somehow change or orient the environment some way, but that's not what you deliver to your customers.

You deliver a set of features, on a release date, with a certain level of defects, for a certain cost. One of those is your driver. The rest are constraints or floats of some sort. See *Manage It! Your Guide to Modern, Project Management* (ROTPM) for more information about how to determine your drivers, constraints, and floats.

Remember, as you consider what's driving your project, you can have only one #1 priority. You might have a right-behind-it #2 priority, and a right-behind-that #3 priority, but you need to know where your constraints and degrees of freedom are.

This is your chance to rank each of the vectors in the pyramid. If feature set is first, fine. If time-to-release is first, fine, if cost is first, fine. If low defects is first, fine. Whatever is first, you don't really care, *as long as you know* and *as long as you only have one #1 priority*. You run into trouble on estimates when your management wants to fix two out of the six sides of the pyramid—or worse—more than two sides.

When your managers say to you, "Here's the team, here's the office space, here's the budget, here's the feature set, and here's the time," you only have defects left to negotiate. And, we all know what happens. The defects go sky high, and you also de-scope at the end of the project because you run out of time. That's because you have too many fixed constraints.

5.3 Insist on a Ranked Backlog

If you really want to estimate a date or a budget, here is how to do it. Make sure you meet these conditions:

1. You must have a ranked backlog. You don't need a final backlog. You can certainly accommodate a changing backlog. But you need a ranked backlog. This way, if the backlog changes, you

know that you and the team are working on the work in the correct order.

2. The team who will do the work is the team who is doing all the estimation. Only the team who is doing the work can estimate the work. Otherwise the estimate is not useful. Surrogate estimators are biased estimators.

3. You report all estimates with a confidence range. If you report estimates as a single point in time, people think your estimates are accurate and precise. If you report them as a confidence range, people realize how inaccurate and imprecise your estimates are, and you have a shot of people treating them as real estimates.

You need a ranked backlog because the order of the features matters. Let's use dinner as an example. If you eat dessert before dinner, you might not want dinner. Why bother estimating how long it will take to make dinner if you're not going to eat it? If you provide some features, and the customer says, "Thanks, this is great. You can stop now," you don't need the rest of the features. You don't need to estimate them, either.

Once you've met the conditions, you can estimate. The same reasoning works for both project dates and budgets.

5.4 The Team Doing the Work Provides the Estimate

Once you have a ranked backlog, make sure the team doing the work estimates its own work. Otherwise the estimate is not useful. Surrogate estimators are biased estimators.

Managers and senior architects tend to underestimate the amount of work. They tend to think the work is easy to do, especially if the requirements are clear.

Other teams might overestimate the amount of work. That's because they are not familiar with the domain, the requirements, the code base, or the tests.

You cannot depend on anyone's estimates except for those of the team doing the work.

CHAPTER 6

How to Estimate

You have options for estimation, once you have met the preconditions. If you don't have the feature set in a ranked order, you are in trouble. That's because if you use any life cycle other than an agile life cycle, the feature order matters to your estimates, and the team will discuss the feature order in addition to the size of the estimates. That will make your estimation time take longer and your team will not agree. It all starts to get stickier and stickier.

The smaller your chunks of work are, the easier it is to estimate. Either create small stories, one or two days long, or create inch-pebbles.

6.1 Your First Best Bet: Make Your Stories and Chunks Small

If you cannot wait to estimate, because someone is breathing down your neck, demanding an estimate, look at your backlog. How small are the stories? Here's my rule of thumb: If you eyeball the story and say, "Hmm, if we put everyone on the team on this story, and we *think* we can attack this story together and get it done in a day," then the story is the right size.

You can add up those stories, which are about one team-day in size, give yourself a 50% confidence level, because you don't really know, and proceed with Use Timeboxes, Better Your Estimate as You Proceed (6.4.1, p. 24).

If someone is breathing fire down your neck, chances are good that no one has taken the time to create a backlog of right-size stories. But, maybe you got lucky. Maybe you have a product owner who's been waiting for you, as a team, to be available to work on this project for the last six months, and has been lovingly hand-crafting those stories. And, maybe I won the lottery.

6.2 Your Second Best Bet: SWAG and Refine

Let's say your manager has asked you for a date and you were unable to get empirical data from the team, so instead you decide to develop a SWAG: a Scientific-Wild-Tush-Guess.

SWAG Suggestions:

- If you must develop a SWAG, develop it with the team. Remember, a SWAG is a guess. It may be an educated guess, but it is still a guess. You want to develop a SWAG the same way you estimate the stories, as a team.
- Develop a 3-point estimate: optimistic, likely, and pessimistic. Alternatively, develop a confidence level in the estimate.
- When you start with a SWAG, also start collecting data on the team's performance that the team—and only the team—can use for the team to use to better their estimation.
- Refine the SWAG: Explain to management that your original date was a SWAG, and that you need to refine the date. I like the word "refine," as opposed to "update." Refine sounds like you are going to give them a better date—as in sooner rather than later. You may not, but no matter what, you will be giving them a better date—as in a more accurate date.

6.2.1 *SWAG No-Nos*

- Do NOT SWAG alone. The team gets to SWAG. It's their estimate, not yours, as a project manager.
- Do NOT let your manager SWAG for you. Unless the manager is going to do all the work, the manager gets no say. Oh, the

manager can decree a date, but then you go back to How to Estimate (p. 21) and manage the project and re-estimate reasonably.

- Do NOT report a SWAG without a confidence percentage or a date range attached.

6.3 Collect Data

In the previous examples, you had some knowledge of the team's velocity. But, maybe you are working on something brand new, with a team new to the domain.

You have no idea how to estimate. All of your estimates will be wrong. What can you do? Gather some data.

6.3.1 *Wait to Estimate Until You Know How the Team Works*

If you have not worked on a project like this with this team, you have other problems. It's not worth estimating the entire backlog at the beginning of the project, because the team members have no idea what relative estimation means to anyone else on the team. The team needs to work together. So, ask them to start together as quickly as possible. Yes, even before they estimate anything. They can work on anything–fixing defects, developing the stories for this product, anything at all. You all need data.

Since you have a ranked backlog, the easiest approach might be to start with a kanban board so you can visualize any bottlenecks. You may want to use kanban inside an iteration, so you have the rhythm of the iteration surrounding the visualization of the kanban.

If you keep the iteration to one or two weeks, you will see if you have any bottlenecks. The shorter the iteration, the more often you will get feedback, the more valuable your data.

Once the team has successfully integrated several features, you can start estimating together and your estimates will mean something. Use the confidence level and re-estimate until the team's confidence reaches 90%. How long will that take? I don't know. That's why you have a kanban board and you're using iterations. I have seen new-to-agile teams take 6–7 iterations before they have a velocity they can rely on at all.

6.4 When You Have a Decreed Date

It's fine to live with a decreed date—that means you get to manage the features. Now, you have a choice. You can work in iterations or in flow (kanban). Let's assume you work in iterations for now.

6.4.1 *Use Timeboxes, Better Your Estimate as You Proceed*

If you *have* worked on a project like this, with this exact team before, you can use this team's velocity. Go ahead and use the team's velocity and estimate the entire backlog with the team. I would timebox this effort to no more than 2 hours total. It's not worth spending any more time on it, because your estimate is bound to be wrong. Remember, this is new work you've never done before.

This estimate is the first date you cannot prove you cannot make. This is your most optimistic estimate. It is not the most likely estimate, nor is it the most pessimistic estimate. Well, unless you are all Eeyore-type people, in which case it might be the most pessimistic. But, I doubt it. I would take that estimate, and say to my manager, "Here is an estimate that I have about 50% confidence in. I will know more at the end of the third iteration."

The team tracks its velocity for three iterations and re-estimates the entire backlog again. The team can re-estimate and compare what it now knows with what it knew before. Now, you have something to compare. You now ask the team how much confidence they have in their estimate. Report that to management. Maybe they have 50% confidence, maybe they have less. Maybe they have more. Whatever they have, report that to management.

Repeat estimating the remaining backlog until you get to 90% confidence.

6.4.2 *When You Have a Decreed Date and a Decreed Backlog*

Some of you are saying, "JR, my manager has also decreed the feature set." Fine. As long as your manager has decreed the feature set in rank order, you can make this work.

You still need to know in what order your manager wants the features delivered. Why? Because if you look back at the Determine Your Degrees of Freedom (5.2, p.17), several things can occur:

1. Your customers/manager may not want all the features if you demo as you proceed.
2. Your customers/manager may not want to pay for all of the features as you proceed, especially if you provide an estimate and demo.
3. You are getting dangerously close to having too many fixed constraints on this project, especially if you have a fixed number of people and a fixed working environment. Do you also have a fixed cost? You are in the danger zone! I can guarantee you that something will not be fixed once your management or customers see the number of defects.

6.4.3 *Obtain Data First, Then Argue*

If the manager has decreed the date and the feature set why are you estimating anything? Get to work!

Use timeboxes or kanban and determine your true velocity and cycle time. You gather this data to understand how long a typical story might take (cycle time), and how many stories you can complete in a timebox (velocity). Even if you only gather data for a couple of weeks, you have more information than if you have no data.

During the project, perform demos to show progress to your management/sponsor/customer. The people mandating what you do have no idea if their decrees/wishes are reasonable. There's no point in fighting with them until you've accomplished a substantial portion of the ranked backlog or worked through one third to one half of the schedule. Once you've completed several features or a significant part of the schedule (to a meaningful milestone), you have data and can see where you are.

Now you can take your data, and Use Timeboxes, Better Your Estimate as You Proceed (6.4.1, p. 24). You can provide estimates for the rest of the backlog with confidence ranges.

When I've been the project manager for imposed dates and imposed backlogs, I've explained to management that we will do our best, and that we will maintain a reasonable pace from the beginning. When we are halfway through the time and the backlog I will report back to management where we are. I then ask, did they want to know where we are a quarter of the way instead, which will give us more flexibility?

That changes the conversation. Sometimes they do, and sometimes they don't. It depends on how crazed the management is. I also protect the team from multitasking (none allowed). I am the Wall Around the Team, protecting the team from Management Mayhem.

6.5 Wrap Up

So where does all of this get us with budgets and dates?

In many ways, estimating project budgets or dates for agile projects turns out to be irrelevant. If you have a ranked backlog, and you finish features, you can always stop the project if you hit a particular date or cost. It does matter if you have a ranked backlog, if you use an agile approach, if you work in flow (kanban), or if you use a life cycle that allows you to finish features (an incremental life cycle where you integrate as you proceed).

That's why I don't get too perturbed when my managers try to fix the schedule and the feature set, and they rank the backlog. They can make the decision to stop the project if we run out of time or money. No problem. We are doing the best job we know how. I don't have to sweat it. Because what matters is the ranked backlog.

To those of you who have programs with large budgets: yes, you do not want to burn through large sums of money without getting value in return. I agree. However, sometimes you don't know if you're getting any value unless you start something and have a chance to evaluate it via a demo to see the value. Your mileage may vary.

6.5.1 *Remember, the Project Is a System*

We discussed this in How to Think About Estimation (p. 15). You have more degrees of freedom than just the feature set or the release date or the cost. You have the people on the project, the work environment, and the level of defects. If you are working on an agile project, expect to iterate on the end date or the budget. You can use rolling wave (p. 32) for agile projects or non-agile projects. Expect to iterate.

Because the project is a system and you will iterate, remember to estimate with confidence levels, both on dates and budgets.

6.5.2 *Determine Your Conditions for Estimation*

With a ranked backlog and knowing how to rank the vectors of your project pyramid, you can take a shot at a first cut at a date or a budget.

Never assume you know what is #1 for your project, #2, and so on. Ask. Sometimes, release date is #1, sometimes it's not. Sometimes cost is #1, sometimes it's not. Just because your manager asks for a release date does not mean that is the top priority. Ask.

If you are agile/lean and you do not have a ranked backlog, you are up the proverbial creek. Do not pitch a fit, but know that you cannot estimate. Explain that calmly and firmly. To everyone. Sure, you can start the project, assuming you have enough ranked stories for one iteration, or enough of a ranked backlog to start a kanban board. You don't have to estimate the project.

In How to Estimate, I suggested these options for when you had some idea of what was going on:

- Iterate on your estimate with timeboxes. If you are using timeboxes, track your velocity. You can re-estimate the backlog and report it as you gain more confidence in your estimate. Go re-read Use Timeboxes, Better Your Estimate as You Proceed (6.4.1, p. 24) for the details.

- Obtain data first. When you have a decreed end date and a decreed backlog, do not argue first. Do not bang your head against the wall. It hurts your head and does not change the situation. (I love it when the people who are not working directly on the project think they know more than you do. This kind of thing happens all the time in program management.) Go re-read Collect Data (6.3, p. 23) for the details.

- Wait to estimate until the team has experience working together. Can you estimate anything without knowing how this team will work on this project? I don't think so. And, you should hedge your bet by keeping your iterations short. Reread Wait to Estimate Until You Know How the Team Works (6.3.1, p.23).

- Keep stories and iterations small. Make the stories small so they are easier to estimate. Make any tasks small so you can estimate them. Make the iterations small so you get feedback faster. Small is beautiful, baby. If you have anything larger than team-day task, you are In Trouble.

- SWAG and refine. Estimate with the team, and plan on refining the estimate. Please do not allow your estimate to be someone else's commitment (a schedule game). Don't forget to read the SWAG No-Nos (6.2.1, p.22).

Those are my suggestions. Confidence percentages help a lot.

You can use these ideas for dates or budgets. Substitute "budget" or "cost" for "date" and you will see that the ideas fit.

I wish I could tell you there was a magic recipe or a crystal ball to tell you how to determine the unknown from no knowledge. There is not. You need data. But it doesn't take long to get the data if you use an agile life cycle. It takes a little longer with an incremental life cycle.

6.6 Estimating a Program

If you need to estimate a program (a collection of projects with one strategic objective), you may say, "These ideas are great, but I have multiple teams' estimates to add together. What do I do?"

For a program, each team does this for its own ranked backlog:

- Take every item on the backlog and roadmap, and use whatever relative sizing approach you use now to estimate. You want to use relative sizing, because you need to estimate everything on the backlog.
- Tip: If each item on the backlog/roadmap is about team-day or smaller, this is easy. The farther out you go, the more uncertainty you have, and the more difficult the estimation is. That's why this is a tip.
- Walk through the entire backlog, estimating as you proceed. Don't worry about how large the features are. Keep a count of the large features. Decide as a team if this feature is larger than two or three team-days. If it is, keep a count of those features. The larger the features, the more uncertainty you have in your estimate.
- Add up your estimate of relative points. Add up the number of large features. Now, you have a relative estimate, which based on your previous velocity, means something to you. You also have a number of large features, which will decrease the confidence in that estimate.

Do you have 50 features, of which only five are large? Maybe you have 75% confidence in your estimate. On the other hand, maybe all of your features are large. I might only have 5–10% confidence in the estimate. Why? Because the team hasn't completed any work yet and you have no idea how long their work will take.

As a software program team, get together, and assess the total estimate. What's the software program team? The software program team is the cross-functional team whose job is to get the software product to done. It's not just the software teams—it's everyone involved in the technical program team. See *Agile and Lean Program Management: Scaling Collaboration Across the Organization* (ROTPGM).

Note: the teams have to trust their delegates to represent them to the software program team. If the teams do not trust their delegates, no one has confidence in any estimate at all. The estimate is a total SWAG.

The delegates to the software program team know what their estimates mean individually. Now, the software program team "adds" them together—whatever that means. Do you understand why we call this prediction? If you have component teams instead of feature teams, they may have to add more buffer time to manage the risk of creating features. Do they have to add time for the experiments as they transition to agile? Do they need to gain the trust of their management? Or, on the other hand, are they already experienced agile feature teams?

The more experienced the teams are at agile, the better the estimate is. The more the teams are feature teams, the better the estimate is. If you are new to agile, or have a mixed program (agile and non-agile teams), you should know that the estimate is way off.

It's time for the software program manager to say, "We have an initial order-of-magnitude prediction. But we haven't tested this estimate with any work, so we don't know how accurate our estimates are. Right now our confidence in our estimate is about 5–10% (or whatever it is). We've only spent a day or so estimating, because we can spend time delivering, rather than estimating. We need to do a week or two of work, deliver a working skeleton, and then we can tell you more about our prediction. We can refine our prediction as we proceed. Remember, back in the waterfall days, we spent a month estimating and we were wrong. This way, you'll get to see product as we work."

You want to use the word "prediction" as much as possible, because people understand the word prediction. They hear weather predictions all the time. They know about weather predictions and its relationship to accuracy. But when they hear estimates of work, even if you use confidence numbers, they think you are accurate. Use the word *prediction.*

6.7 Beware of These Program Estimation Traps

There are plenty of potential traps when you estimate programs. Here are some common problems:

- The backlog is full of themes. You haven't even gotten to epics, never mind stories. I don't see how you can even make a prediction. That's like my saying, "I can go from Boston to China on an airplane. Yes, I can. It will take time." I need more data: which time of year? Mid-week, weekend? Otherwise, I can only provide a ballpark estimate, not a real estimate.
- Worse, the backlog is full of tasks, so you don't know the value of a story. "Fix the radio button" does not tell me the value of a story. Maybe we can eliminate the button instead of fixing it.
- The people estimating are not the ones who will do the work, so the estimate is full of estimation bias. Just because work looks easy or looks hard does not mean it is.
- The estimate becomes a *management* target. This never works, but managers do it all the time. "Sure, my team can do that work by the end of Q1."
- The people on your program multitask, so the estimate is wrong. Have you read the Understanding Multitasking and the Cost of Delay on Estimation (p.89)?

Managers think they can predict team size from the estimate. You might be able to add more teams and/or people. You cannot guarantee a larger team or more feature teams will meet an estimate, or decrease the time needed. This is the problem of splitting work in the mistaken belief that more people make it easier to do more work. More people make the communications burden heavier.

Estimating a program is more difficult, because bigness makes everything harder. A better way to manage the issues of a program is to decide if it's worth funding in the project portfolio. Then, work in an agile way. Be ready to change the order of work in the backlog, for teams and among teams.

As a program manager, you have two roles when people ask for estimates. You want to ask your sponsors these questions:

- How much do you want to invest before we stop? Are you ready to watch the program grow as we build it?
- What is the value of this project or program?

You want to ask the teams and product owners to deliver results:

- Please produce a walking skeleton (of features in the product) and build on it.
- Please produce small features, so we can see the product evolve every day.

The more the sponsors see the product take shape, the less interested they will be in an overall estimate. They may ask for more specific estimates (when can you do this specific feature?), which is much easier to answer.

Delivering working software builds trust. Trust obviates many needs for estimates. If your managers or customers have never had trust with a project or program team before, they will start asking for estimates. Your job is to deliver working software every day, so they stop asking.

Now you know how to estimate. There is more.

CHAPTER 7

Rolling Wave Planning

Project teams can use rolling wave planning to deliver interim milestones and then replan the next chunk of the project.

Here's how rolling wave planning works:

Loop:

- Plan what you know for the next few weeks (I use a 3–4 week rolling wave). If you're managing a traditionally planned project, make this as detailed a Work Breakdown Schedule (WBS) as you like. If you're managing an agile project, you may not have to do any more planning than what you already have done.
- As each week goes by, use the knowledge you've gained about the project to replan the already-planned weeks and plan the next week at the end of the current schedule.

Endloop

As the project proceeds, you'll replan frequently, but you won't replan a lot of the work.

7.1 Learn as the Project Proceeds

The idea behind rolling wave planning is that you can't know everything about the project in advance, so don't bother trying to plan a lot in detail. Plan the next few weeks in detail, always staying about three to four weeks ahead of the project. In my experience, it's not worth trying to look more than four weeks ahead. Things will change too much.

Of course, if you know you have hard dates like end-of-quarter or a trade show, put those events in the schedule. But rolling wave planning is much more likely to help you achieve those hard dates.

I incorporate adaptive planning into my rolling waves, by using the knowledge I've gained about the project to (re)organize the work as necessary.

If you haven't tried rolling wave planning, give it a shot. I find it especially helpful when I want to timebox to meet a specific date and I want an early warning if the date is impossible.

CHAPTER 8

There Is No Correct Estimation Model

For years, we bought the cone of uncertainty for estimation—that is, our estimates were just as likely to be over as under.

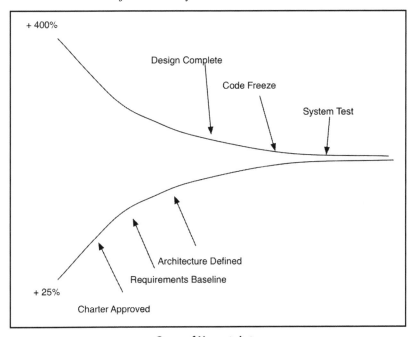

Cone of Uncertainty

Laurent Bossavit, in *The Leprechauns of Software Engineering* (BOS), shows us how that assumption is wrong. (It was an assumption that some people, including me, assumed was real.)

This is a Gaussian (normal) distribution. It's what we expect. But, it's almost never right. As Laurent says,

"Many projects stay in 90% done for a long time."

What curve do our estimates follow if they don't follow a Gaussian distribution?

Troy Magennis, in *The Economic Impact of Software Development Process Choice—Cycle Time Analysis and Monte Carlo Simulation Results* (MAG), suggests we should look at the Power-Law (Weibull) distribution.

What this distribution says with respect to estimation is this: We are good at estimating small things. We get much worse with our

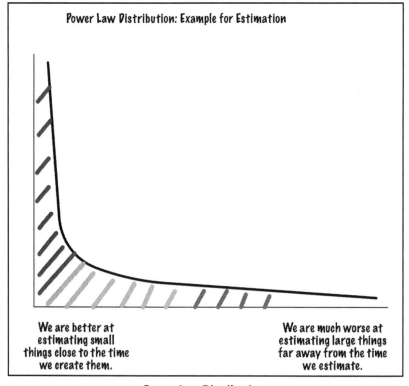

Power Law Distribution

estimation quickly, and for the long tail (larger and larger chunks of work), we are quite bad.

Why? Because creating software is innovation. Building software is about learning. We better our learning as we proceed, assuming we finish features. Maybe take another look at Software is Learning, Not Construction (p.11).

8.1 We Invent; We Don't Repeat

We rarely, if ever, do the same thing again. We can't apply precise estimation approaches to something we have never done before.

The question is this: What effect does understanding an estimation model have on our estimates?

If we know that the Gaussian (normal) distribution is wrong, then we won't apply it. Right, why would you do something you know to be wrong? You would not estimate large chunks and expect to have a +/- 10% estimate. It doesn't make sense to do that.

But what can we do? In Troy's paper, he says that if you have large, unique work items or you have large WIP, you will have poor predictability.

My suggestions for your estimation:

- Estimate small chunks of work that a team can complete in a day or so.
- Keep WIP low.
- Replan as you finish work.
- Watch your cycle time.
- No multitasking.

What should you do when people ask you for estimates? What kind of requirements do you have? If you have large requirements, follow my advice and use the percentage confidence, as in Estimating a Program (6.6, p. 29).

You can predict a little for estimates. You can refine your prediction. And, you may have to predict a large effort. In that case, it helps to know what distribution model might reflect your estimate.

CHAPTER 9

But I Need to Know When the Project Will Be Done

I was talking with a new-to-agile project manager, who said he needed to spend the first iteration to do design and estimation. I asked why. "Because our management needs to know exactly when the project will be done," he said.

"Do you think your iteration of design and estimation will provide you with a perfect estimate?"

"Uh." He paused. "From your question, I'm guessing you don't think it will."

"I have never found that spending two weeks will provide a perfect estimation for anything larger than a 2-week project. But I could be wrong. Have you been able to do this before?"

"No."

"Oh. Do you think you can get a perfect estimate this time?"

"No."

"Then why would you spend your time doing an estimate instead of producing something, learning from that, and bettering your gross estimate?"

"Because my manager needs to know when the project will be done!"

I *feel* for this guy. I do. I understand why his management wants an estimate that's better than a SWAG. But you can't always give your managers what they want. You might be able to give your managers what they need (with apologies to The Rolling Stones).

9.1 What You Can Say to Managers Who Think They Need to Know

If you are starting a project and you are using iterations, you can do a gross estimate of the entire backlog, do one iteration, track your velocity, and guess at how many more iterations you will need. Your guess is dependent on the backlog not changing, on your gross estimate being right, and on your initial velocity being a predictor of future velocity. Put like that, your managers will realize your initial estimate is a guess, and they may very well want another estimate in another iteration or two or three. That is a very good thing. You can do that.

If you are not using iterations, you can do a SWAG, understanding that your estimate is wrong, until you have some delivery of some sort. Until you have some part of your product working, you will have no idea how far off your estimate is.

If you prefer to use kanban, that's fine, as long as your features are minimum marketable features. If your MMFs are *maximum* marketable features, you will have no idea when you can be done because you are not limiting work in progress. Kanban is great for limiting work in progress for the entire team, and for not piling up work where people can't finish it. The team can't proceed until the *team* finishes work.

Once you have data, you can forecast when the project will be done. If that's after several timeboxes, great. If that's after some number of minimum marketable features, great. But you can't really provide an estimate *without* data. Otherwise, it's just a SWAG. And if you want a SWAG, I can give you a SWAG. It won't mean anything, but I can give you one.

CHAPTER 10
NoEstimate or Do Your Estimates Provide Value?

There's a discussion in the agile community around "NoEstimates." This is not literally "*no* estimates," but the ability to work in small-enough chunks and show progress so that you don't need estimates.

In many agile projects, teams spend time using planning poker or t-shirt sizes to determine the relative size of a chunk of work. Planning poker works like this: Using the Fibonacci series, 1, 2, 3, 5, 8, 13, etc., everyone on the team decides how big this piece of work is. If you use t-shirt sizing, you use XXS, XS, S, M, L, XL, XXL.

To use either planning poker or t-shirt sizing means the entire technical team doing the work decides together what the relative size of a feature is.

I don't like sizes larger than 2 for Fibonacci series, or XS for t-shirt sizing. Why? Because the feature is probably multiple stories. I want stories—those chunks of work—to be something the team can complete in one day or less. I can live with two days.

There are many reasons for this:

- We have research that says we like to finish work in small chunks so we can make progress. See *The Progress Principle: Using Small Wins to Ignite Joy, Engagement, and Creativity at Work* (AMA).
- The larger the chunk, the less opportunity we have to get feedback as we proceed. We might spend an entire week (or more) on work that has no value.

- The more the team finishes, the more the Product Owner, and the other interested managers see the progress and remain engaged.

In estimating, I have found that discussion about the stories is great. I have not found that relative estimation is worth the time—except to say, "This feature is too large. How do we break it apart?"

If you spend time on your relative estimates, and your team is not completing a story every day (more is better)—or in the worse case, every other day—you are wasting your estimation time. Spend time on learning to break the stories apart, rather than in estimation.

When you create small stories that the team finishes fast, you create a flow of value through the team. The estimates don't create value. Finished work does create value. That's what you want.

Consider whether your estimates create value. If not, what could you do instead? Consider the ideas in We Invent; We Don't Repeat (8.1, p. 37).

CHAPTER 11

Use All Four Parts of Project Estimation

What if you're not agile? You need to track your estimate and refine it over time.

Project work estimation has three components: the initial first cut, or a SWAG; tracking the estimate against the actuals; and using the schedule to see what's happening in your project.

If you've been assigned project estimates, or if your project estimates aren't particularly close to reality, don't fret. Try these techniques to estimate and learn about your estimates.

11.1 Part 1: Create an Initial Estimate

If you're a project manager, you probably try to estimate the work at the beginning of the project, even if you're assigned a project end date. Sometimes, senior managers have trouble hearing what you've said in your estimate. I use one of these three options for creating estimates for the entire project:

1. Provide a date range for the estimate: "We'll be able to release between May 1 – June 15." Some senior managers can't hear the second half of that statement: they only hear May 1. If you work for a manager like that, try either of these other two suggestions.
2. Use the word "about" to describe the precision of the estimate: "5 people for about 9 months or 10 people for about 6 months." You haven't described an end date, but you have explained something about the people and time you'll require.

3. Provide a confidence level to describe the range of dates: "I have 90% confidence in June 1 and 100% confidence in August 1." In my experience, even the managers who can't hear the "between" estimate can hear my confidence levels.

Once you have a gross estimate at the beginning of the project, you can drill down and create estimates for each of the project components. Whether you try to create precise estimates, or choose to use slack buffers to deal with incomplete estimates, you will have some project estimate.

The problem with estimates is that they are guesses. They're the best guesses we can make, as good as we can make them, but they are still guesses. As the project unfolds, you will be able to acquire feedback on how well you estimated and to know how to update your estimates, with the second part of estimation, the EQF, Estimation Quality Factor.

11.2 Part 2: Track Estimation Quality Factor to Understand the Project Estimate

As you continue to manage the project, track your initial completion date estimate. Each month, or in a short project, each week, take 5 minutes out of your project team meeting, and ask: "When do you think we will finish the project?" Track that estimate on a chart set up with the release dates on the Y-axis, and the date that you asked the question on the X-axis.

There are two good reasons for asking this question. First, you continue to focus your project staff on completing the project. People tend to work on what you, the project manager, focus on. Second, by asking your project staff, you can discover the various confidence levels the staff has in the release date. When you look at the EQF chart, you can see if people are concerned that the project will *not* meet its release date, or if they are feeling confident about meeting or *beating* the release date. Then you can deal with their concerns or your concerns.

When you track EQF with your project team, you're learning more about the project and using EQF to learn how good your initial estimate was.

11.3 Part 3: Use EQF to Manage Project Concerns

I use the slope of the EQF to ask questions like, "Tell me what's happened in the project to make you think we will meet/beat/miss the date." When people become more optimistic or pessimistic, I want to know why. The EQF not only gives me feedback on my initial estimate, it also gives me another technique to discuss the project state with the project team.

And, once I understand the project team's concerns, I can either deal with them or elevate those concerns to my management.

11.4 Part 4: Update Your Estimate as You Know More

When you first created an estimate, you developed some date range, an "about" date, or a series of dates with a confidence level. Once the project is underway and you're using EQF to understand what the rest of the project team thinks of the date and the risks to the project, you're ready to update your project estimate.

If the team has missed interim milestones and all of you think there is no way to deliver the requested feature set in the estimated time with appropriate defect levels, then it's time to slip the project. Remember, don't slip a week every week; that's an out-of-control project. Instead, make the slip as long as you need it. Manage the risks of further slippage by creating more interim deliverables.

If the team has met their milestones, and you're on track, you can close in on a more specific date. For example, if you started with a completion date of "May 1 – June 15," about halfway through the project you might be able to say, "May 8 – June 10." About three quarters of the way through the project you can probably say, "May

20 – June 1." As you reach May 1, you can say when in those ten days you can complete the project.

Every project worth completing has some project uncertainty. EQF is a great technique for displaying project uncertainty and understanding why the project team is uncertain about the project.

The more everyone understands about the project, the better your project management will be, and the more likely you are to meet your SWAG. At least, you'll know how far off your SWAG was, and why. And that knowledge can help you on your next project.

CHAPTER 12

Show Your Status and Update Your Estimate

Sometimes, you need to explain where you are in the project, and when you expect to be done to other people. Consider a probabilistic estimate.

Make sure you don't fall into the 90% Done schedule game. (See *Manage It! Your Guide to Modern, Pragmatic Project Management* (ROTPM) for a large list of schedule games, including the 90% Done game.)

And, when are you done? You can stop a project if there is no more value, or you've run out of time, money, or people.

Let's take each of these.

12.1 Probabilistic Scheduling

When I was writing *Manage It!*, I had no idea how far along I was. My editor and publisher wanted to know when I would be done.

When I write, I have several phases: the exploratory phase, where I write articles, the write-it-down phase, where I write the whole thing down (in chunks, of course), and the editing phase. They asked me in the write-it-down phase. In this phase, I need hours at a time to blast away at a chapter until there's little enough of it left so I can write it in spurts.

The question was this: when would I be done with the first draft, the write-it-down part? I explained that I had a slim chance of being done by mid-October, and a stronger chance of being done by Thanksgiving. Here's the graph of what that looks like:

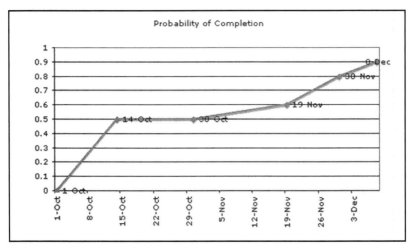

Probable Completion

Note that there's a 50% chance I'll be done with this phase, the write-it-down phase, by mid-October. I have a bunch of writing time between now and then for the book. I have some other writing to do, some website updates, etc., but most of my time is available for writing the book. If I miss mid-October, I have no writing time until almost the middle of November. That's why if I'm close in mid-October, I might be able to finish in mid-November. But if I miss mid-October because I'm not close, the mid-November date is quite risky. I have a bunch of writing time from mid-November through early December, but I expect to be traveling again and teaching, which changes the availability of time for writing.

This is an example of probabilistic scheduling. I don't even have a 100% completion date (which you might have to have for one of your projects), because I will be replanning in mid-October, no matter what. Any 100% date I give now will be wrong, wrong, wrong. It will either be too optimistic or too pessimistic, and I won't know which one until October.

It doesn't matter what kind of life cycle you use, the further out the dates are, the less you know. You can use probabilistic scheduling to help you, the project team, and your sponsors see the risk in the schedule.

CHAPTER 13

Refocusing: 90% Done Is Not Almost Done

Back when I was a new developer, my boss asked me how long it would take to complete a specific task. I looked at it for about 20 seconds, and said "Four weeks." "Great," he said.

At the end of the first week, I was 25% done—that's what I reported on my status report. At the end of the second week, I was 50% done.

At the end of the third week, I was 75% done. At the end of the fourth week, I was 90% done. At the end of the fifth week, I was 92% done.

At the end of the sixth week, when I reported I was 92.5% done, my manager finally took pity on me.

"Johanna, do you know *when* you will be done?"

"Nope. Not a clue."

"Would you like a little help learning how to know when you'll be done?"

"You bet!"

My manager knew that 90%, 92%, and especially 92.5% done was not anywhere near done. Rather, it was a good clue that I had no idea *when* I would be done. I'd run smack dab into the 90% Done syndrome.

My manager sat me down and asked me questions that helped me break the large tasks into many smaller tasks. Like most people, I'm good at estimating smaller tasks and not so good at estimating larger tasks. Then, I listed all the test cases I would have to check to know if this code was done. I didn't call them test cases back then; I called them "done criteria." My boss and I both knew that once I'd finished the tasks and made sure my code met the "done criteria," I would actually be done.

That work took me almost ten weeks to complete. Luckily, I had an understanding manager who helped me plan and test my way out of the 90% Done syndrome.

Here are actions you can take, whether you are the one stuck in 90% Done or the manager of a person stuck in 90% Done:

1. List everything you need to do, to finish the big chunk of work. I include any infrastructure work, such as setting up branches in the source control system.
2. Estimate each item on that list. This initial estimate will help you see how long it might take to complete the entire task.
3. Now, look to see how long each item on that list will take to finish. If you have a task longer than one day, break that task into smaller pieces. Breaking larger tasks into these inch-pebbles is critical for escaping the 90% Done syndrome.
4. Determine a way to show visible status to anyone who's interested. If you're the person doing the work, what would you have to do to show your status to your manager? If you're the manager, what do you need to see? You might need to see lists of test cases or a demo or something else that shows you visible progress.
5. Since you've got one-day or smaller tasks, you can track your progress daily. I like to keep a chart or list of the tasks, my initial estimated end time, and the actual end time for each task. This is especially important for you managers, so you can see whether the person is being interrupted and therefore is multitasking. Check out my article about the Split Focus schedule game.[1]

---

[1] http://www.jrothman.com/pragmaticmanager/2008/06/refocusing-emerging-from-the-split-focus-schedule-game/

Sometimes, people fall into 90% Done because they're implementing across the architecture, writing all the GUI, or writing all of one layer at a time. If you shift people to implementing by feature and have them work in short iterations, they start trying to estimate and complete smaller chunks of work. Their estimates will be more accurate, and they are more likely to finish the work.

CHAPTER 14

Future Fixes

A reader recently asked me, "When planning a project phase, how do you account for the bugs that you know will be created? Do you simply create a "bug bucket" and hope you put enough time in it? Or is there a better way?"

Yes. Allotting a random amount of time for rework is better than assuming it doesn't exist, but predicting rework—how much your project will require and when it will end—is tricky. I use several techniques to predict rework, depending on the project and the organization's culture: allowing each task to complete without incurring extra rework; predictive measures such as historical data and estimation quality factor; and planning and managing the project schedule using critical-chain project buffers or agile techniques.

14.1 Plan Ahead

To reduce or plan accurately for rework, first make sure you're not creating more of it. Under pressure to meet their estimated dates, a project team may complete the development of as much of their code as possible by their scheduled date, and then open defects against their own code. (I call this incurring technical debt.) This team increases their need for rework by at least one order of magnitude. Why? Because they don't complete the work when it's fresh in their minds (the developers move on to the next task), so they leave half-baked software for other people to attempt to use in their development. When these downstream developers run into trouble with their software and can't finish on time, they'll open defects against the code, and march on toward the next task.

When the original team returns to complete their work, they find incomplete code and they've forgotten some of the important issues about it because of the time elapsed between their initial implementation and the rework. Trouble ensues.

If your project artificially meets deadlines when developers say, "The feature is complete, but there are a few things I need to take care of later," stop. The project won't meet the deadline—not if you know there are defects or incomplete work in the code. Avoid creating more rework by completing tasks, including all associated repair, testing, documentation, and any other work necessary to complete the task before going on to the next task.

If you can avoid creating extra rework, you can use predictive measures to determine when the rework is complete. The three measures I use are historical information, estimation quality factor, and fault feedback ratio.

14.2 Hindsight is 20–20

To use historical information, gather data from a few previous projects. I gather such stats as the number of team members, the total project duration, the size of the project (lines of code and the number of requirements), and the percentage of the total project duration that was rework. I also gather defect trends throughout the project: how many defects were open, closed, and remained open per week, so I can understand the previous projects' profiles.

Then I ask a few questions about the project itself. How similar is it to any of my previous projects? Can I use previous data to predict this project's rework effort, or should I scale it up or down due to the relative size of my current undertaking? By the same token, I review defect trends in each project to see if the defect profile still looks similar. If the defect trends look similar, I can continue to use the historical rework information.

If you've shortchanged the product in the past and incurred technical debt from not completing the product in past releases, the historical information is only a starting point. You'll have to increase your rework estimate to account for technical debt work before you can apply it to this project. You'll have more rework because you're not starting from a stable base, and the developers may not remember why they took shortcuts.

14.3 Track Your Estimates

Whether or not you have historical records, you do have information about this project once you start it. Throughout the project, I use estimation quality factor (EQF) to track the overall schedule estimate and estimates with each developer. See Use All Four Parts of Project Estimation (p. 43).

In his book *Controlling Software Projects: Management, Measurement, and Estimation* (DEM), Tom DeMarco suggests you track the overall schedule estimate by periodically estimating when you think the project will end. I use this technique with the project team together and with individuals for their tasks.

At each project team meeting, I ask people to predict when the project will be complete. If the team trusts each other and me, they tell me verbally. If there's not a lot of trust, I ask them to write the end date on a sticky note. I then graph the dates on a flip chart and see where they fall.

More often than not, the developers and testers have a realistic estimate of when they will complete their tasks. Based on the answers, I ask these questions:

- What have you seen or heard (or not seen or heard) that makes you think we'll finish later?
- What have you seen or heard (or not seen or heard) that makes you think we'll finish earlier?

You can ask the questions without the data, but then the discussion soon dissolves into a shouting match: The person who screams the loudest decides when the project will end.

In addition, when I'm managing a high-stakes project with a tight schedule, I ask each developer and tester to track each of their tasks' EQF. If they can't make progress at the project's beginning (tasks take more time than anticipated), I know early on that we're in trouble—and that gives me more time to implement a reparative process.

14.4 Measure Bad Fixes

While planning the project, or by using historical data and EQF during implementation, you can reliably predict the amount of rework necessary. However, starting with the work products, to predict the effect of bad fixes on rework progress, you can measure the fault feedback ratio (FFR): the number of bad fixes to total fixes. Even in the requirements, analysis, and design phases of a traditional project, assuming that you track defects, you can see how many defects cause other problems or can't be closed on in the first attempt. If the developers have trouble in the initial phases, ask them if they think they've resolved the problems, or if they'll have more trouble once they hit the coding phase. This gives them an opportunity to tell you if they're resolving unknowns in the early phases, or if the requirements are so vague that they still can't figure out what's going on.

Especially in the coding phase, if the developers are spinning their wheels with a high FFR, they can't make progress. Maybe it's time to refactor, just to make the code clearer, or perhaps it's time to redesign, reduce coupling, and increase cohesion—or change modularity. But whatever the problem is, you must first understand that there is a problem, so you can work with the project team to determine what to do.

I find FFR especially helpful during final system test. One of my project teams thought they'd met their schedules all along during the project, but during the final system test, they kept running into problems. At one point, they thought they were slipping a week every week—but I thought they were slipping two weeks every week because the defects uncovered significant design issues. Their FFR was 20 percent—indicating that one fifth of all fixes either weren't really fixed or caused other problems. They instituted peer reviews on all fixes and brought the FFR down to less than 10 percent, which allowed them to predict an end to the project.

14.5 Manage Your Buffers

Sometimes, rework seems excessive because the project wasn't scheduled accurately. If everyone estimates his or her tasks using the first possible date that a task is complete, assuming that the planets align and Murphy's Law doesn't squash your project, your project won't meet its schedule. When that happens, it appears that rework has taken over the project—but that ain't necessarily so, to paraphrase the immortal Ira Gershwin. Many people estimate project duration by predicting the duration of each task plus a buffer, or "fudge factor." However, fudge factors allow project staff to wait before starting a new task, even if they finish a task early. And sometimes, fudge factors just aren't hefty enough.

Separating the task estimates from the fudge factors can help to schedule the project to allow for rework during each task or in the planning stage. When I plan a project, I ask team members to estimate their tasks, keeping the fudge factor separate from their reasonable estimate. (A task estimate then looks like 80 hours plus 16 hours of buffer or fudge factor.) Then I gather all the individual task buffers from the critical path into one comprehensive buffer at the end of the project. If a task on the critical path takes longer, I remove that time from the comprehensive buffer. If a critical path task completes earlier and people start on their next task earlier, I add that extra time to the buffer. During the project, I monitor the buffer. If it empties faster than I expect, I know that the task estimates are incomplete. If the buffers empty at about the right time, we're on target for both tasks and rework.

14.6 **Incorporate Agility**

Agile techniques offer immediate feedback to developers, helping to create fewer defects and less rework. If you can, incorporate agile techniques such as test-first development, automated unit testing, and pair programming—or at least another pair of eyes reviewing the code.

If you've got a large project with several agile teams and you're not sure if you're really going to catch all the defects in each iteration, plan on a defect search-and-fix mission on one iteration before you release it to the customer. Planning for one iteration of contingency is reasonable, especially if you think your project is risky due to size or newness to agile techniques. And if you're using agile techniques, one iteration should be more than sufficient for detecting and fixing defects.

Developers create code—and defects. But shoving them under the rug isn't the solution. If you don't mask the real schedule by saying a task is complete when it's really not or by making the developers context-switch, they'll create fewer defects, and fix the ones they do generate with a reasonable rework plan.

Using historical information, EQF to help you analyze the schedule, and FFR to determine your developers' stress and accuracy level, you can predict, plan, and manage necessary rework activities. Critical-chain buffer management can help you reduce risk and glean early insight into the project schedule. Finally, agile techniques can help developers improve quality while they code rather than after the fact.

Guessing at rework with a "bug bucket" is better than nothing—but not much. A wiser approach is to get a clear view of the necessary fixes in your future—and then fit them into your schedule.

Troubleshooting Your Estimation Problems

You know your estimates are guesses. They will be wrong. Here are some ideas for actions you can take to prevent estimation problems or when you realize your estimates are wrong.

CHAPTER 15

Avoid Multitasking

Let's talk about the effects of multitasking on estimation.

Many managers want people to work on several projects at one time. This is the multitasking problem. I've said before that multitasking introduces defects. We have research that says it makes you stupid. Still, some managers don't want to manage the project portfolio and assign people or teams to projects. They think people can work on multiple projects at one time. We still have multitasking.

What can you do?

In *Manage It! Your Guide to Modern, Pragmatic Project Management* (ROTPM), I said you shouldn't even bother estimating when people are multitasking. Why?

- You have no idea when people will be available to work. A person might estimate a task will take four hours. But, if they need to spread those four hours over five days, you have no idea when that person can deliver the results you want.
- Your project will incur a delay. The more multitasking, the more delay you will have.
- You can't tell how much context switching people have when they multitask. That four-hour task might take eight, because it takes so much time to return to the context.

When you have people multitasking, you cannot estimate with any accuracy.

If you are using estimates to decide which projects to do, you can see that your estimate is wrong, and does not provide you useful information.

Worse, if you incur a cost of delay because your team members are multitasking, you won't realize the value of the project when you work on it and finally release it.

Multitasking is not just the quickest way to waste a team member's time, it makes it impossible to estimate with any accuracy. Even if your ideal time is accurate, the duration cannot be accurate.

If you want an accurate estimate, make sure the project team members are full time on one project at a time.

CHAPTER 16

Avoid Student Syndrome

Student Syndrome occurs when the person with the task waits until the last possible moment to start. Some people spend their entire academic career waiting until the night before a project is due and then starting it, pulling an all-nighter, and getting some (hopefully adequate) grade. Student Syndrome isn't for me, but I know lots of people who do this.

I use these techniques to avoid Student Syndrome:

- Ask each person to develop inch-pebbles so that person (and the project manager, if necessary) can track progress.
- Use Estimation Quality Factor to continuously predict the end of their current task (not just the end of the project).
- Ask "What have you completed today?" Just asking can help jiggle people into starting the work.

These techniques work for me too, not just when I manage other people. Just because I don't wait until the last possible moment doesn't mean I don't procrastinate every so often. (In English, that means I procrastinate too :-)

Student Syndrome isn't the same as being stuck, although if I'm stuck, it can look like I'm procrastinating instead of working on the task. I use a timeout to see if I'm stuck. For any given task, if I can't make progress on it in about 30 minutes, I ask for help. Thirty minutes may be too short or too long for your tasks, so adjust accordingly.

If you're a project manager or a functional manager, notice if your staff are waiting until the last possible moment to start. If so, try something to help people start earlier. Late-as-possible starts lead to late projects.

You most often see Student Syndrome on non-agile projects. You *can* see Student Syndrome on agile projects where each person takes a backlog item individually—or when people multitask.

When people take backlog items individually, try these ideas:

- Pair or swarm on each backlog item. Reduce the team's WIP.
- Make each item small, so a person can finish it in one day.
- Decide on a team norm about what to do when people get stuck on work. How long can they remain stuck without asking for help?

If someone is multitasking, understand why. Multitasking makes everything late and creates a cost of delay in your project.

CHAPTER 17

Estimation Units Predict Schedule Slippage

I've been teaching a project management workshop, and one of the participants said something brilliant: "If you estimate in days, you'll be off by days. If you estimate in weeks, you'll be off by weeks." If you estimate in months, you will be off by months.

Here's why. The more you can break a big task apart, the more likely you are to remember all the pieces and estimate each piece well. The less you know about a task, the more gotchas you'll encounter, and the longer the task will take. And, the bigger the task, the more likely you are to fall into Student Syndrome (p. 63).

If you're a PM and you don't understand why your schedule is slipping, look at the general task duration. Got a lot of week-long tasks? Or multiple-week-long tasks? Those tasks are slipping, and you won't know why or by how much until the time is almost done. I bet your project will slip for a duration of several of those multi-week tasks. Replan now, breaking all those tasks into inch-pebbles.[1] Then you'll have a much better idea of what it will really take to finish this project. And maybe, just maybe, you won't have that much of a delay, because delays of weeks are very different than delays of days.

Does small planning take time? Yes. That's why I recommend rolling wave planning (p. 33) so you don't have to do lots of estimation at one time. Or, if you're agile, you know you don't do a lot anyway.

---

[1] http://www.jrothman.com/papers/howinch-pebbles.html

Remember, you can't estimate epics, large compound features. They are too large. You need to break them apart into small features.

CHAPTER 18

Edit Those Epics

I've been working with folks making their transition to agile. In this process, I've discovered transitioning to agile is hardest for managers and technical leaders.

Managers are accustomed to working in timeboxes. To them, the iteration is a timebox. But, they also are accustomed to features spanning multiple timeboxes, and that's not OK in agile.

They are accustomed to predicting the end of the project, and they now want to use the team's velocity and the story sizes to predict the end of the project. That's OK, but it's not always wise. It assumes nothing will change, but agile is all about fast change. The managers' fixed mindset is bumping up against the technical team's change mindset.

This leads me to a root cause. If you think your job is prediction, you don't change the size of the stories, and that means the stories are too big. The stories are *epics*.

It's fine to start with epics—very large stories. But, in order to have releasable product at the end of an iteration and to keep iterations short enough to get feedback often enough, you need small stories. That means you'll start with epics and decompose them into stories. At first, this seems impossible.

Here's one way to start. What's the first valuable thing—the smallest chunk that delivers business value to the customer, to the developers, to the testers, to *someone*—that we can do that we can show to someone at the end of a short iteration? Is that small thing a story? Is it small enough to be completed inside an iteration, maybe by the entire team? If so, complete that story in the iteration. If that thing is not a story, what would make it a story? If it is not small enough, can you decompose it further?

Making stories small enough to finish in a one- or two-week iteration is a common stumbling block for many teams in their transition to agile. Until a team can do that, they can't move to agile. They can't take advantage of kanban either, because their stories are too big—nothing will move across the board.

This thinking challenges several assumptions on the part of managers and technical leads:

- That there is *one and only one* right person to do *that* work. I'm not saying people are fungible. I'm suggesting members of a team swarm around the work.
- That work has to follow a specific order. I'm not saying the work is order-less. I'm suggesting you may have more flexibility than you think at first glance.
- That work has to be a big huge chunk in order to be done. I know that you can work in inch-pebbles. You have to do something first. You have to do something next. I know this.
- That work must only benefit one persona. I'm suggesting work can benefit not just the eventual customer, but also the developers, the testers, the marketing people, the trainers, and even HR or legal. Please do not start your stories with "As a customer." Which customer?

Managers and technical leads are accustomed to thinking big about projects. They have needed to, in the past, because their managers asked them to estimate the entire darn project or, even worse, the entire program to see when it might end. They think they need to know velocity now to estimate the entire project. They still might.

But, they can't do that if stories span iterations. They can only be successful if the teams complete stories inside iterations. Teams cannot get partial credit for stories. Partial credit perpetuates work in progress, which is a *very bad thing*, no matter what agile or lean approach you are using.

If senior management needs to know how long the entire project will take, the best way is still to explain, "We need three iterations to be able to estimate. We will track our velocity for three iterations and give you a reasonable three-point estimate at the end of that time, OK?"

Anyone who won't wait six weeks, or three two-week iterations, for a reasonable estimate wants a SWAG. In that case, you can say, "Christmas," and don't provide a year. This is the "Happy Date" schedule game. You give them what they want to hear, because reality will intrude soon enough.

If you are transitioning to agile, here are guidelines I have found useful:

Make your stories small enough so that you, the team, can finish more than one story inside an iteration. My rule of thumb is that you should be able to complete a story every day or, at worst, every two days. If you can complete stories more often, that's even better. If you can't complete a story at least once every two days as a team, your stories are too big. Yes, there are exceptions, but you'd better have a darn good reason.

Remember that velocity is personal to a team. As soon as you change a team's makeup, velocity can change. So, don't change the people on a team if you want any sort of predictability about estimation.

If you really want some predictability, make the stories really small, so that people can pair on them and still finish them in a day or less. Then, all you need to do is count the stories to have a rough idea of how long the team needs to finish the project. "That's a lot of stories, JR!" Of course it is. That's why you're paying people to work on the project.

I no longer estimate my work. I make sure my chunks of work are tiny. That way, I just keep chugging along. That would work for your team, too.

But, whatever you do, give up the notion of stories spanning iterations. If your stories are big enough that they need to span iterations, stop right there. Stop with the partial credit. Put those stories on a diet. Separate the stories—not into tasks, but into multiple, independent, smaller stories that the responsible person or product owner can schedule into the most appropriate iteration and rank when it's time for that story to be implemented.

CHAPTER 19

What You Can Do For Estimation

In But I Need to Know When the Project Will Be Done (p. 39), I talked about what you can do for estimating an agile project (do a gross estimate of the backlog, estimate your velocity, better your estimate every iteration, and keep talking to your management). What if you have a contract? What if your managers really do need to know exactly when the project will be done? What if you *don't* have an agile project?

Let's take these one at a time. If you have a contract, that date is your release criterion. By definition, you will be done. What's the problem? If you rank your product backlog, get to done at the end of each iteration, or make sure each feature is really done when it works its way off your board, what is the problem? I don't understand the question. Really, I don't.

When your date is fixed, your scope can change. If you have a fixed date, fixed scope where is the flexibility in the project? In *Manage It!* (ROTPM), I ask you to ask the sponsor, "If it's 3 weeks before the end of the project and we don't quite have everything in the project, and we have too many defects, what decision are you going to make: keep going until we have everything in, fix the defects, or release anyway? Let me know now, and I'll know how to make tradeoffs."

If your managers need to know exactly when the project will be done—ask "Why?" There is probably a good reason, such as there is an important project waiting to start right behind this one. This is a good thing, because it means your managers are managing the project portfolio. There might be another reason, such as a sale depending on this project. You want to learn why, because you might be able to help whatever that dependency is without a lot of drama. You might not, but you might. You can't help if you don't know why.

Now, the hardest one: if you don't have an agile project. This is hardest, because it's hardest to see progress as you proceed, so your estimates are likely to be wrong. And, if people are multitasking, your estimates are guaranteed to be wrong, and you will be maximally slow, and Murphy will not just visit you on this project, he and his extended family will live with you forevermore.

But, if you don't have an agile project, you still have options. You don't have to use a serial life cycle. Sure, you can say you're using whatever life cycle your organization says to use. But, they pay you to manage risks and be a project manager. So, if you say, "In order to manage risks on this project, I am going to iterate on the architecture three times to test the architecture with three features and then give you an estimate that we think is within 50% of reality," are they going to say "No"? No, they might say, "50%, we need to know within 5%!!" And then you can say, "Great, here's how I'm going to tell you that."

The problem is that at the beginning of the project—any project— you have too much uncertainty to provide any exact estimate. An estimate is a guess. You need to evolve any estimate over time. My favorite estimation technique for a non-agile project is to spiral in on a date. At the beginning of the project, you say, "Somewhere in this quarter." For this example, let's call it Q1.

As you proceed, you say, "Somewhere around the middle of Q1." Some smart-aleck manager says, "Oh, Feb 14?" You say, "NO, it's not a Valentine's Day present. There's a plus/minus here. Call it anywhere from late January to late March. That means the absolute earliest it could be is late January, but I have little faith it could be late January. And, even I think it will be before late March. But I don't know where in the middle of Q1 it will be. I can update you with a better estimate next quarter, when it's September, OK?"

The problem is you need that smart-aleck manager to listen to your entire paragraph. Otherwise, the manager only hears himself, and not you, which is a potential problem.

The key is you have to use iterative planning and tracking approaches, incremental development, and I recommend you use continuous integration, because otherwise you get to the end and you get surprised, which is a *horrible* feeling. I wrote an article about this a number of years ago, called Use All Four Parts of Project Estimation (p. 43).

Exact estimates are an oxymoron. Estimates that you update? Those are useful. I can't understand why any manager wouldn't want those.

CHAPTER 20

Estimation Depends On...

I taught my estimation workshop twice last week and once the week before, and one thing remains true: Estimation depends on the project life cycle, how the project is organized, the state of the requirements, and the number of people you have available.

I used a number of simulations to help people see how to estimate, and I noticed a number of interesting effects:

- In the public workshops, people were more willing to experiment and live with a different life cycle for a simulation (a more concurrent life cycle, or an iterative or incremental approach).
- In the on-site workshops, the participants recreated their environment, even when they said they wanted to try something new. Goes to show you how difficult it is to change.
- Relative sizing is a great way to account for the difference in capabilities caused by not having specialists or people with subject matter expertise. ("A 2 for this group is more time than a 2 if we had a so-and-so.")

I encouraged people to try incremental and agile approaches to their projects in the workshop. The participants agreed that the approaches provided faster results, but were still concerned that they would not be able to implement those approaches at work. Some of the people were so accustomed to not having enough people, that even when I asked, "How many people for how long?" they could only assume they had access to the other one or two people in their small groups, even though we had 20 people in the room.

Yes, we encountered Parkinson's Law (work expands to fill the time allotted), which is why I timeboxed the estimation time. "But we need more time for estimation!" "Do you get that time from your managers?" "No." "So, maybe you can try some other approaches to make your estimates better in a shorter period of time?"

We discovered that non-functional requirements are more difficult to estimate than user stories or even use cases. And, it still amazed me that people are given broad brush requirements, and are then supposed to generate an accurate estimate (within 10%) with such little data. Yes, we talked about ways to iterate on your estimate to refine it. Will their managers listen? I don't know.

We even had an opportunity to test out my claim: Multitasking nullifies all estimates. See Avoid Multitasking (p. 61).

It never fails. When I teach an on-site workshop, some people think their work is more important than the workshop. Maybe it is. But I do know that when they leave and arrive and leave and arrive, it mimics what they do at work, and slows down their project. Because I break everyone into parallel groups, when they return, they can see the effect of their in-and-out behavior on their project.

When you estimate, make sure you think about how the project is organized, how many people you need when, and what information the requirements provide. Then show a confidence graph or a three-point estimate to explain how the estimate is really a guess, but a good guess, not a SWAG.

CHAPTER 21

Estimating Testing Time

Partway through an assessment, the senior manager asked me, "How long should the testing take?"

The answer to the senior manager's question is, "It depends."

If you do test-driven development, there is rarely more than an iteration's worth of at-the-end testing. When I coach teams who are transitioning to test-driven development, I recommend they plan for one iteration at the end of the project for final system test and customer acceptance test.

Once the team has more experience with test-driven development, they can plan better. I have found there is always a need for some amount of customer acceptance testing at the end. The amount of testing time varies by project and how involved the customers were all along. If you're using an agile life cycle even without test-driven development, I recommend starting with one iteration's length of final system testing—but just one iteration.

I am assuming that the developers are fixing problems and refactoring as necessary during an iteration, which is real agile development, not code-and-fix masquerading as agile.

But I suspect many of you are not yet using agile life cycles with short iterations.

If you're using any of the following:

- an incremental life cycle such as staged delivery where you plan for interim releases (even if the releases aren't to the customers)

- an iterative life cycle such as spiral or evolutionary delivery
- a serial life cycle such as phase gate or waterfall

Then planning for testing is difficult because it depends so much on what the developers provide, and you won't know until you start testing.

I'd expect as much testing time as development time, but it doesn't have to come all at the end as final system test like it looks in the waterfall pictures. Any proactive work you do-such as reviews, inspections, working in pairs, unit testing, integration testing, building every night with a smoke test, fixing problems as early as they are detected---can all decrease the duration of final system test. If you're the project manager, ask the developers what steps they are taking to reduce the number of defects they create. If you're the test manager, work with the project manager and the developers to create a set of proactive defect-prevention practices that make sense for your project.

Wherever you are in the organization, recognize that final system test includes several steps: testing the product, finding defects, and verifying defects. Your first step is to separate these tasks when you estimate the duration of final system test.

One question you should be able to answer is, "How long will one cycle of 'complete' testing take?" We all know we can't do complete testing, so your version of complete is the tests you planned to run and any other exploratory tests or other tests you need to run in one cycle of testing to provide enough information about the product under test. I realize that's vague and depends on each project. I don't know how to be more explicit because this is a project-by-project estimate. If you work with good developers, the cycle time can decrease a bit from the first cycle to the last—because the testers know how to set up the tests better and the product has fewer defects, which allows the testing to proceed faster.

Once you know how long a cycle of testing takes, estimate how long it will take the developers to fix the problems. I use this data:

- the number of problems found per cycle in the last project,

- my gut feeling for how many more/less we should find per cycle in this project,
- and bug-tracking system data telling me the average cost to fix a defect pre-release.

If I knew that the first cycle in the last release found 200 problems, that it took the developers half a person-day each to fix the problems, and I have ten developers, I estimate ten working days to fix problems. That's a long time. And yes, I was on a project where that's what it took. It was agonizing—we thought we'd never finish fixing problems.

Now that you know how long a cycle should take, estimate the duration for fixes after the first cycle. How many cycles of testing do you plan? When I set up projects, I tend to use some proactive defect detection and prevention techniques, so I generally plan on three cycles of testing. A number of years ago, in a casual conversation with Cem Kaner Ph.D, Professor of Software Engineering at the Florida Institute of Technology and the Director of Florida Tech's Center for Software Testing Education and Research, he mentioned a product for which he planned on eight cycles of testing. For one project, for which I was a contract test manager, we had almost thirty cycles of testing. I can't tell you how many cycles of testing you'll need because that depends on the product's complexity, how good your tests are, and the initial count of product defects before the project started.

Here's what I have noticed from my work with multiple organizations. The groups who want to decrease testing time tend to perform the least proactive work reducing the overall number of defects, and they typically perform primarily manual black box testing at the end of a project. I understand their desires, but they've set up their life cycle and processes to produce exactly the wrong result.

The best guess I have is to estimate the number of cycles you'll need for testing, the duration of one cycle, and the time it takes for developers to fix problems between cycles. Add up the testing plus fixing/cycle and multiply by the number of cycles you think you'll need, and you'll have an estimate of the testing time needed.

By the way, when I do this, I _never_ give a single number; I always give time per cycle ("It will take us six days per cycle"), my estimate of the number of cycles ("We'll need four cycles"), and my estimate of defect-fixing and verification time ("Plus three days between test cycles for developers to fix problems"). That way I can show the costs of not performing proactive defect prevention in a nice way. And I can show my uncertainty in my estimation ("That's a minimum of thirty-six working days, longer if the defects take longer to fix and verify").

If you want to reduce testing time and create a low-defect product, test all the way through the project with a variety of test techniques. Use test iterations so you know at the end of one test cycle where you stand with defects. The lower the number of defects and the more sophisticated your tests, the faster your testing time.

CHAPTER 22

Need to Learn More About the Work You're Doing? Spike It!

In a recent estimation workshop, one of the participants asked, "How do we estimate something we've never done before?"

"Is it a feature or a project?" I asked.

"A feature," she said.

"How do you do things now?" Based on her previous comments in the workshop, I suspected she was pretty good at what she did.

"I take a little time, do a proof of concept, and then I know how long the rest of the work will take."

That's the general idea of a spike. You timebox a little work, do some research—just enough to know how long it will take to finish the rest of the work—and then you can estimate the rest of the work.

22.1 How Does a Spike Work?

I like to timebox the spike for these reasons: You don't want this to become a research project that never ends. If you can't gain some answer in a reasonable amount of time, that's data, too. If you learn enough before the timebox is up, you can stop early. And you might want to explore in a different direction if you have extra time. Maybe you've only tried one design and you want to try another.

But that leads me to my second point about spikes. When you have multiple people work on spikes together, you have options to explore multiple designs. You don't waste time, and you learn together.

Spikes are for learning. There's always a tradeoff between the time you spend learning and actually completing the work. The more time you spend learning, the closer you are to completing the work, so it's important that you timebox the learning. You don't want the learning to go on and on and on ... You might go off into uncharted territory and do something unrelated. No, in a spike you want to stay focused on the problem under research.

In the same way, because you are learning, you want to share that learning with other people. If you're the only one who understands the proof of concept, you have to explain it in words. That's where code or tests can come in mighty handy.

Back in the workshop, my participant described how she used a proof of concept to explain a particularly gnarly piece of security code prototype to a colleague.

"It wasn't until we both got in there and went through it line by line that he understood it. By explaining it to him line by line, I understood it better, too. It's almost as if we had a code review on it together."

I asked, "What if you had paired on it?"

"That might have been even better. He would have had suggestions as I wrote it. I bet it would have been better."

22.2 Spikes Are About Learning

Because spikes are about learning, it makes sense to use all of your learning techniques during them. I'm a big fan of pairing during spikes. When you work with another person, you may discover, as I have, that your work is different—and, often, better.

You might use TDD (test-driven development) also—not to make the code better, although that might happen. When you use TDD, you drive the design through tests. The tests inform your design. The tests suggest alternative questions and drive your learning.

You might also consider BDD (behavior-driven development) as an option. Again, this might make your code better, but that's not the point. The point is to see what happens with your experiments and learning.

22.3 What Happens to the Code at the End of the Spike?

You've timeboxed your experiment. You have a proof of concept and you have a prototype or something you can show other people. They like it and say, "Wow, that looks great! Let's use it. Pop it in the system and be done with it."

Now what?

You have to say, "No, it's a proof of concept; an experiment. It's got holes a mile wide in it. It doesn't account for all of these cases," and then you name several. "It needs real testing. I did an experiment." Maybe you even experimented with another developer or tester, but the code isn't done. If you put that code into the system, you'll create technical debt up the wazoo. What do you do?

You can throw out the code. You can use the code as a basis for real development. Or you can refactor the code to get to something reasonable. It all depends on where you start. Any of those will change the estimate of how long the rest of the work will take.

Whatever you do, you will need to estimate how long the rest of the work will take. But you have the learning from the original timebox. You have feedback from your users or product owner and part of your team. You know enough to explain to the team what this feature will take and where the risks are, or you know enough to do another spike.

22.4 "Use the Code As Is…"

After a spike, I bet many of you hear, "Use the code as it is. It's good enough. You can refactor it in the future." That's enough to make anyone concerned about planning for spikes.

Your code might be quick and dirty because you planned to throw it away. Your code might be a small proof of concept that is very narrowly implemented and would be very hard to refactor. You could do it, but the cost would be high.

The idea is that you use the learning from your spike, not your code. If you can use your code, great. But that's not the goal.

22.5 How Many People Were Involved in the Learning?

The real question is this: How many people were involved in the spike? The more people in the spike, the more people were involved in the learning—and the more easily those people will be able to estimate the real work.

A couple of years ago, I consulted to a team about a difficult performance issue. Because their entire product was based on performance, they weren't sure what to do. They thought it was a process problem, which is why they asked me to help.

In a sense, it was. I suggested they spike their problem and spend no more than one day as a team researching it. When they met the next day at their standup, they each had much more data. Now, they could begin formulating a solution.

They developed three candidate algorithms as developer pairs. That took two days. They developed five different test scenarios as a team, then automated the tests in tester-developer pairs. That took them two more days. They could now spend one more day running the tests against their candidate algorithms.

After one team-week, they had an answer. It was not the answer they expected, but they had the data they needed to know how to proceed. The entire team had been involved, so when the product owner said, "Just use the code," the entire team could say, "No, we need to evolve the design and the tests," and explain why.

Spikes aren't for everything. But when you need to do research and discover what's going on, they work. Put them in your estimation toolbox and see what you learn.

CHAPTER 23

Use Targets as Estimates

Your organization wants you to complete a project (or a feature or task) by a specific time or within a specific cost. That specific time or cost is a target.

You need to be careful about the number of targets you accept. You *can* use both time and cost as targets, as long as you don't constrain anything else in the project. See Determine Your Degrees of Freedom (5.2, p. 17). If you have more constraints, you are over-constraining your project.

23.1 How to Use Targets

You can use project targets to meet the deadline or budget.

Depending on how far away the target is, you can do these things:

- Timebox everything. It doesn't matter what project life cycle you use. Timebox everything. That way you never have to worry about work taking longer than it should.
- Use deliverable-based milestones. Deliverables are working product. With deliverables, you can see the product unfold.
- Divide the target into at least monthly deliverables. You may want a deliverable every week or two if the target date is within six months. As the project team delivers the interim product, you can use Estimation Quality Factor to predict how close you will be to meeting the target.
- Never allow multitasking.

I can't guarantee you will meet your target. However, this approach will enable you to see your product in progress. You can change what you do next as you monitor the progress.

23.2 When the Target Is a Trap

Don't fall into these target-as-estimate traps:

- Your first estimate is the target. Your first estimate is when you know the least about the project. If that is your target, make sure you use the tips above.
- The target is very close, as in a couple of weeks, and you don't know enough about the requirements of the project to use the target well. Instead, you want to spike the work. See Need to Learn More about the Work You're Doing? Spike It! (p. 81).
- Never commit to features and a target. You can say, "We will meet the target. But I can't guarantee how many features we will have by that target." Walk your sponsors around the project pyramid. See How to Think About Estimation (p. 15).

In some ways, it's easier to manage to a target. As long as you are seeing deliverables periodically, you can change what you do, to manage the risks.

CHAPTER 24

How to Avoid Three Big Estimation Traps

I bet there are times you need to estimate how large your project or program will be, at the gross level: "It's bigger than a breadbasket. It's smaller than a person on the moon." More likely, "It's about x people for about y months with this percentage confidence." Or, you use a date range, as I suggest in *Manage It! Your Guide to Modern, Pragmatic Project Management* (ROTPM).

But that doesn't mean you won't fall into estimation traps. Here are three big traps I've seen:

Trap 1. Someone wants you to estimate a large program, and they think that estimate is good forever and ever, amen.

Ahem. Times change. People change. Technology changes. The platform changes. Why wouldn't your estimate change, too? Consider delivering your estimate with an expiration date: "This estimate will expire in 60 days."

Trap 2. You thought this backlog item was small. Instead, it turned out to be something you needed to spike.

Murphy's Law happens on projects and programs. Sometimes, your estimates are just guesses. What's the best thing you can do? Expose them as guesses as fast as you can. Then, manage the risk.

Estimates have built-in variability. The smaller you make your stories, the less variability you will have. And, every so often, something will still surprise you. Or, you will say, "We need to spike this, because we have no idea what this beast is."

Trap 3. Someone wants you, as an agile program manager, to add up all the estimates from the agile project teams and "commit" to when the program will be done.

If you have started an agile program, you have several options, but adding together relative estimates is not a good idea. Relative estimates mean that one team's t-shirt sizing is different from another team's poker planning, which is different from another team's ability to swarm around features in flow, and not bother estimating at all.

But what do you do with a reasonable request from your management?

- You can create a product backlog burnup chart, instead of an estimate.
- You can ask, "How much do you want to invest before you want to stop investing, to manage the money risk?"
- You can say, "Please explain what risks you want to manage, and I will explain how we, as a program, are managing them." Your management does need to know what you will deliver, and when. Seeing your progress in the form of demos and burnup charts might help more than estimates.
- You may even want to ask, "What value do you want to see before we stop? We might be able to provide a SWAG in a short time for that. The value might be an MVP (Minimum Viable Product). It might be more than an MVP. The key is to help your managers help you by focusing them on the value you will create. That way, you won't fall into any of these traps.

CHAPTER 25

Understanding Multitasking and the Cost of Delay on Estimation

Sometimes, you don't have short projects, so projects get backed up, and your managers ask you to work on several things at once. Or, the managers can't decide which project is #1. Somehow, you end up doing several things "at once." This is the multitasking problem, and this is the cost of delay.

You know me, I hate multitasking. The costs are significant. But those are just the costs of multitasking on the work you are doing now. That has nothing to do with the cost of delay to your projects.

In *Manage It! Your Guide to Modern, Pragmatic Project Management* (ROTPM), I have this nice picture of what happens when you try to multitask between two projects.

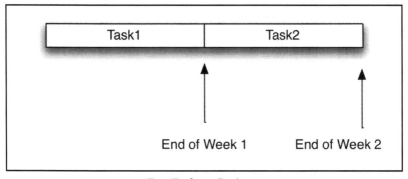

Two Tasks or Projects

Imagine you have two projects. Each of them should take a week. For illustration purposes, I'm making them short.

You can deliver one of them at the end of the first week. You can deliver the second one at the end of the second week.

But, imagine you have to multitask between them. Instead of being able to deliver anything at the end of the first week, you can't deliver anything at all until the second week. And, depending on how much context switching you do, you might not be able to deliver anything until sometime during the third week. The blue boxes show the time lost due to context switching.

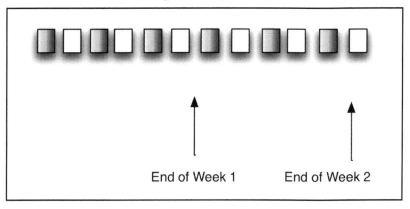

Effect of Multitasking Delay to Delivery

This is a huge cost of delay due to multitasking. This is why you cannot provide an accurate estimate with multitasking. You have no idea when people will work on which project, or how long their context switch will take.

How do you calculate this?

Just saying "Big" is not quantitative enough for some people. This is where using some of the tools from the people who do this for a living might be good.

I've always drawn a back-of-the-napkin picture like the Cost of Delay and explained, "I don't know how to estimate the time in the blue boxes. The blue boxes are the delay times. I can't estimate

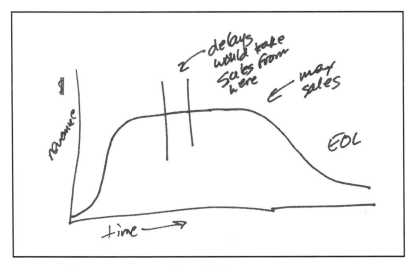

Cost of Delay

them, because everyone else is delayed by multitasking on their projects, too. Sometimes, it takes me an entire day to get an answer to a question that should only take me an hour to get an answer. All I know is that "ideal" time is irrelevant to "actual" time. And even calculating using relative estimation is hopeless. That's because we are multitasking. All of our estimations are out the window because we are multitasking.

"The amount of time we spend working on a project might be accurate. It's the wait time that's killing us. I don't know how to estimate that."

Here is something to try: Take a two- or four-week window, and ask people to write down their predictions of what time they thought some task would take. Then, I ask them to write down, as they spend their time on each task, how much time they actually spend on each task. Now you can compare the prediction to reality.

Remember that all of the context switching and wait time is the time you need to remove from the maximum sales revenue, had you released the product.

This is very difficult to do. It saps the morale of the people doing the work. They quickly realize how often they go back to the same thing, over and over and over again, making zero progress, trying to realize where they are. Do not do this for more than a four-week window. If you must do this, label this an experiment to obtain data. Explain you are trying to obtain actual work time, context switching time, and wait time. Let people label the time as they will.

The managers will be astonished by how little time the technical staff spend on real work. They will be amazed by how much time the technical staff spend on context switching and wait time. This is why managers think technical staff are bad at estimation. Who can be good at estimation when they are multitasking?

The problem is this: the cost of delay due to multitasking is *real*. It's invisible to most people, especially management. It's not just the cost of the blue boxes in the picture above. It's the fact that nothing gets out of your organization until the end of Week 2 or later. Remember what the Cost of Delay looks like? Even if you use that calculation, you can see you are losing revenue left and right due to multitasking.

Remind the managers: Remember that all of the context switching and wait time is the time you need to remove from the maximum sales revenue, had you released any of the products.

Can you use this as an argument for your managers to end the multitasking and manage the project portfolio?

Cost of delay due to multitasking is real. Multitasking changes your project estimation so you cannot predict anything. Don't let multitasking affect your estimates.

CHAPTER 26

What You Know About Estimation Now

We've examined estimation for agile and non-agile projects. We've talked about preconditions, what to do when things take longer, and how to make your work smaller.

Let's summarize what you can do to make your estimates better.

26.1 Transition to an Agile Approach or an Incremental Approach for Your Projects

When you finish a feature, which you do in agile or incremental life cycles, you understand what it took to achieve this feature. You can use the knowledge garnered from that achievement to understand how to estimate better for the future.

If you use a serial life cycle (waterfall or phase-gate), you never finish anything until the end. Do yourself a favor, and move to an incremental life cycle. That will allow you to finish features faster.

If you use an iterative life cycle, you can build prototypes and iterate on them, making them better and better. That works for technical risk. It doesn't work that well for project risk, which is what the estimates are supposed to do.

To learn more about life cycles and how to use them effectively, please take a look at the chapter and appendix in *Manage It! Your Guide to Modern, Project Management* (ROTPM).

26.2 Make Your Features Small

If you are using an agile approach, make your features (or stories) no longer than one or two days to finish.

If you are not using an agile approach, use inch-pebbles, so you have a miniature milestone every day or so.

You will be able to see your progress and see when you are stuck. Small stories or inch-pebbles also allow you to do rolling wave planning.

26.3 Iterate on your Estimate

Don't assume you have one estimate and it's great for all time. Projects change. Requirements change. Maybe even the people on the team change.

Make sure you tell people when your estimates expire. If they need another estimate, create a new one.

26.4 Don't Multitask

Multitasking is the fastest way to get nothing done. Don't do it. Manage Your Project Portfolio (ROTMYPP) instead.

26.5 Don't Let Defects Dictate Your Estimate

If you fix your defects as you proceed, you will have a much more accurate estimate. Don't allow your defects to make your schedule slip a week each week at the end of the project.

26.6 Final Thoughts

So that's it. Don't estimate (guess) if you don't have to.

But that's not life. Most of us will have to. Use the techniques described here to make the best guess you can, based on the best data you can collect, and help your managers understand that this is exactly what it is: your best guess for right now.

Now get to work!

Glossary

Agile: You work in small chunks, delivering working software that is valuable to the customer in the order the customer specifies. The value of working in an agile way is that you have the ability to change feature ranking (what you do when) fast.

Backlog: A ranked list of items that need to be completed for the product.

Burnup Chart: A chart that tracks progress towards completion.

Done: How you know a feature is complete and ready to release.

Estimate: Literally, "guess." How long or how much you think the project will take for date and/or cost.

Estimation Quality Factor: Feedback on how good your estimates are.

Fault Feedback Ratio: The ratio of bad fixes to good fixes.

Inch-pebble: Inch-pebbles are one-to-two day tasks that are either done or not done.

Incremental or Incremental Life Cycle: A project approach in which you work by feature or feature set, finishing them as you proceed.

Iteration: A timebox in Scrum. The team completes and releases work at the end of the iteration.

Iterative Life Cycle: An approach where you continually refine the features.

Kanban: Literally the Japanese word for "signboard." A scheduling system for limiting the amount of work in progress at any one time.

Lean: A pull approach to managing work that looks for waste in the system.

MVP: Minimum viable product. What is the minimum you can do, to create an acceptable product? This is not *barely good enough* quality. This is shippable product. However, this is minimal in terms of features.

NoEstimate: A hashtag on Twitter that refers to the team's ability to maintain a stream of releasable work, so you don't need estimates. The estimates don't provide value; the work does.

Pairing: When two people work together on one task.

Phase-gate: A serial life cycle. When you use phases and gates, you have specific decision points. At each point, you are supposed to re-estimate the entire project so you know if it's useful to continue. The difference between this approach and an agile approach, is that in traditional phase-gate projects, you have documents at each milestone, not finished features.

Preconditions: What you need to know before you can estimate.

Serial Life Cycle: A waterfall or phase-gate approach. You proceed with requirements, analysis, design, implementation, code, and test, in that order.

Spike: A timebox where the team investigates and learns more of the details of the feature or story.

Stories: An agile feature, used to describe the requirements of a product. It's called a story because each story describes the value or benefits the team proposes to deliver to the user.

Swarming: When the team works together to move a feature to done — all together.

Target: A project end date or cost that someone picks for you.

Technical Debt: A metaphor referring to the inadequacy of the current system. Some people also call *incomplete work* technical debt. We use the metaphor because the debt will cost us more to fix later.

Timebox: A specific amount of time in which the person will attempt to accomplish a specific task.

Waterfall: Serial life cycle. A sequential design process. You proceed with requirements, analysis, design, implementation, code, and test, in that order.

WIP or Work in Progress: Any work that is not complete. When you think in lean terms, it is waste in the system. You want to eliminate waste wherever you discover it. Note that you do not get credit for partially completed work in agile.

References

[AMA] Amabile, Teresa and Steven Kramer. *The Progress Principle: Using Small Wins to Ignite Joy, Engagement, and Creativity at Work.* Boston: Harvard Business Review Press, 2011.

[BOS] Bossavit, Laurent. *The Leprechauns of Software Engineering.* Leanpub, 2012.

[MAG] Magennis, Troy. *Process Choice — Cycle Time Analysis and Monte Carlo Simulation Results,* in The Economic Impact of Software Development, 2015.

[DEM] DeMarco, Tom. *Controlling Software Projects: Management, Measurement and Estimation.* Prentice-Hall, 1986.

[ROTPM] Rothman, Johanna. *Manage It! Your Guide to Modern, Pragmatic Project Management.* Pragmatic Bookshelf. 2007.

[ROTMYPP] Rothman, Johanna. Manage Your Project Portfolio: Increase Your Capacity and Finish More Projects. Pragmatic Bookshelf, 2009.

[ROTPGM] Rothman, Johanna. *Agile and Lean Program Management: Scaling Collaboration Across the Organization.* Practical Ink. 2015.

More from Johanna

I consult, speak, and train about all aspects of managing product development. I have a distinctly agile bent. I'm more interested in helping you become more effective than I am in sticking with some specific approach. There's a reason my newsletter is called the "Pragmatic Manager"—that's because I am!

If you liked this book, you might like the other books I've written:

- *Agile and Lean Program Management: Scaling Collaboration Across the Organization*[1]
- *Diving for Hidden Treasures: Discovering the Value in Your Project Portfolio* (with Jutta Eckstein)[2]
- *Manage Your Job Search*[3]
- *Hiring Geeks That Fit*[4]
- *Manage Your Project Portfolio: Increase Your Capacity and Finish More Projects*[5]
- *Manage It! Your Guide to Modern, Pragmatic Project Management*[6]

---

[1] http://bit.do/ALPM

[2] http://bit.do/ppvalue

[3] http://bit.do/myjs

[4] http://bit.do/hgtf

[5] http://bit.do/mypp

[6] http://bit.do/manageit

- *Behind Closed Doors: Secrets of Great Management* (with Esther Derby)[7]

In addition, I have essays in:

- *Readings for Problem-Solving Leadership*[8]
- *Center Enter Turn Sustain: Essays on Change Artistry*[9]

I'd like to stay in touch with you. If you don't already subscribe, please sign up for my email newsletter, the Pragmatic Manager,[10] on my website. Please do invite me to connect with you on LinkedIn,[11] and follow me on Twitter, @johannarothman.

I would love to know what you think of this book. If you write a review of it somewhere, please let me know. Thanks!

---

[7] http://bit.do/BCD

[8] https://leanpub.com/pslreader

[9] https://leanpub.com/changeartistry

[10] http://www.jrothman.com/pragmaticmanager/

[11] https://www.linkedin.com/in/johannarothman

Index